Precious Moments

Storybook Bible

This book belongs to

Maia hill

Given by   Date

Mommy

Occasion

Children of Promise

We have such high hopes for our children. We bathe them, feed them, and search for the right clothes. We put them in schools where we believe they will best grow. We treat them with special delights, simply because we long to see the smiles on their faces. We love them. We want the very best for them, and we're willing to make whatever sacrifices we need to ensure that no good thing is withheld from them. And we wait. We hope. We pray that these children of promise will eventually fulfill their God-given destiny.

But what do we really want for our kids? Is it to be rich? Famous? Athletic? Scholarly? While none of these are wrong in themselves, they all fall short of the purpose and meaning to which God intends His children to experience. As much as we love our kids, God loves them more. He wants to give them the very best that there is in this life—and that best is God Himself.

As parents, we have an incredible opportunity—and calling—to introduce them to God and His Word. To let them know God longs to walk with

them all the days of their lives. And you can help cultivate this relationship by praying for and with your children, and by reading the truth of God's Word to them. It is the one investment you make as a parent that you can know will pay rich dividends in the end.

God promises. His Word never returns void. It accomplishes exactly what God intends, every time it goes forth. That's why the Precious Moments® Storybook Bible is so exciting. Yes, it's a beautiful book, filled with all the adorable Precious Moments® characters you and your children have come to love. The illustrations alone will leave your children captivated, waiting to hear what other special stories hide within its pages. But beyond a children's storybook, this precious keepsake is actual Bible text. The stories are excerpts from the International Children's Bible® translation, not a paraphrase. So when you gather your young ones around you to read them a Bible story, you are literally reading to them God's Word, accurately translated into words your children can easily understand. As they grow older, they will find the text just as easy to read as it is to hear.

They will be entertained, for sure, and educated in Bible truths at the same time. But more than that, as God assures us, they will be changed. They will remember the sweet faces and the truths that they illustrate. God's Word will be hidden in their tiny hearts, and it will grow with them, in them, and shine its light through them. Then, as they become parents themselves, they can take this same Bible, open its pastel-painted pages, and pour the love of God into their children, too, continuing the rich spiritual heritage that began around the rocking chair in your home. *The Precious Moments® Storybook Bible* is a beautiful way to introduce your young ones to a personal relationship with God, and a precious reminder of God's faithfulness that you can lovingly pass down to future generations.

God
Bless our
Happy
Home

family

Grandmother _____
                              Name

_____
        Birthday   Place

Grandfather _____
                              Name

_____
        Birthday   Place

Mother Camilla hill
                              Name

_____
        Birthday   her   Place

Me Maya Laren hill
                              Name

14   her
        Birthday   Place

Tree

Grandmother

_____
Name

_____
Birthday   Place

Grandfather

_____
Name

_____
Birthday   Place

father _____gaveh'hLL_____
Name

_____LH_____nere_____
Birthday   Place

Brothers and Sisters

_____   _____   _____
Name   Birthday   Place

_____   _____   _____
Name   Birthday   Place

_____   _____   _____
Name   Birthday   Place

_____   _____   _____
Name   Birthday   Place

Church

Special Ceremonies
(Baptism, Dedication, Christening, First Communion, Confirmation . . .)

Ceremony	Date
Ceremony	Date
Ceremony	Date
Ceremony	Date
Ceremony	Date

Church & Sunday Schools Attended

Church	City	Date
Church	City	Date
Church	City	Date

Record

Vacation Bible Schools

Church	City	Date
Church	City	Date
Church	City	Date

Church Camps

Church	City	Date
Church	City	Date
Church	City	Date

Church Outings

Outing	Event	Date
Outing	Event	Date
Outing	Event	Date

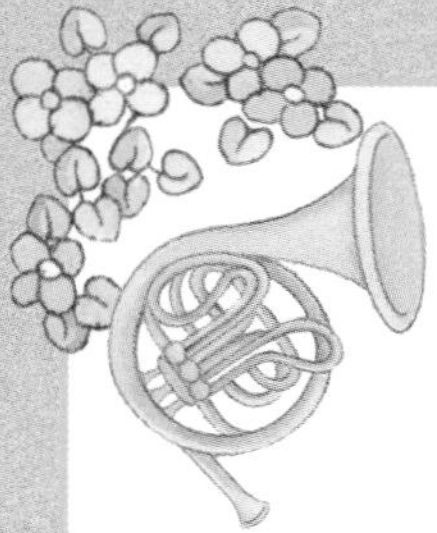

My Favorite Things

Favorite _____   Favorite _____
Places _____   Foods _____

_____   _____

Favorite _____   Favorite _____
Pets _____   Toys _____

_____   _____

_____   _____

Favorite _____   Favorite _____
Games/Sports _____   Stories/Songs _____

_____   _____

_____   _____

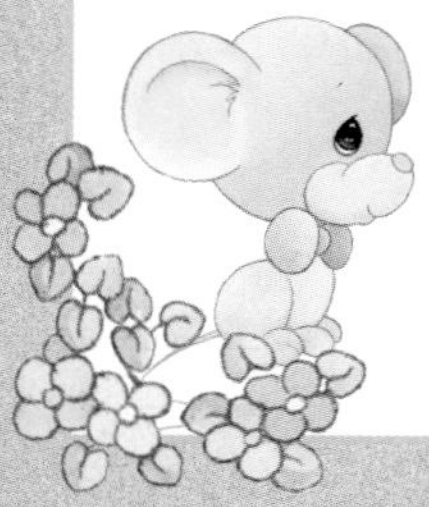

Table of Contents

Favorite Bible Classics

Words of Praise and Wisdom

More Stories of the Faith

Songs and Prayers

Favorite Bible Classics

The Story of Creation

(From Genesis 1 and 2)

[1:1] In the beginning God created the sky and the earth. ²The earth was empty and had no form. Darkness covered the ocean, and God's Spirit was moving over the water.

³Then God said, "Let there be light!" And there was light. ⁴ᵇHe divided the light from the darkness. ⁵God named the light "day" and the darkness "night." Evening passed, and morning came. This was the first day.

⁶Then God said, "Let there be something to divide the water in two!" ⁷So God made the air to divide the water in two. Some of the water was above the air, and some of the water was below it. ⁸God named the air "sky." Evening passed, and morning came. This was the second day.

^{9a}Then God said, "Let the water under the sky be gathered together so the dry land will appear." ¹⁰God named the dry land "earth." He named the water that was gathered together "seas." God saw that this was good.

¹¹Then God said, "Let the earth produce plants. . . ." And it happened. ¹³Evening passed, and morning came. This was the third day.

^{14a}Then God said, "Let there be lights in the sky to separate day from night."

¹⁶So God made the two large lights. He made the brighter light to rule the day. He made the smaller light to rule the night. He also made the stars. ¹⁸ᵇGod saw that all these things were good. ¹⁹Evening passed, and morning came. This was the fourth day.

²⁰Then God said, "Let the water be filled with living things. And let birds fly in the air above the earth."

²¹ᵃSo God created the large sea animals. He created every living thing that moves in the sea. . . . God also made every bird that flies. ²³Evening passed, and morning came. This was the fifth day.

²⁴Then God said, "Let the earth be filled with animals. And let each produce more of its own kind. Let there be tame animals and small crawling animals and wild animals. And let each produce more of its kind." And it happened.

²⁶ªThen God said, "Let us make human beings in our image and likeness."

²⁷So God created human beings in his image. In the image of God he created them. He created them male and female. ²⁸ªGod blessed them and said, "Have many children and grow in number. Fill the earth and be its master."

³¹God looked at everything he had made, and it was very good. Evening passed, and morning came. This was the sixth day.

[2:1] So the sky, the earth and all that filled them were finished. ²By the seventh day God finished the work he had been doing. So on the seventh day he rested from all his work. ³God blessed the seventh day and made it a holy day. He made it holy because on that day he rested. He rested from all the work he had done in creating the world.

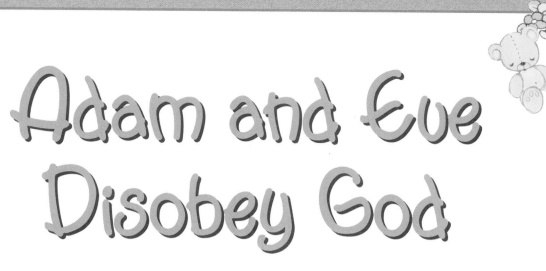

Adam and Eve Disobey God

(From Genesis 3)

[3:1] Now the snake was the most clever of all the wild animals the Lord God had made. One day the snake spoke to the woman. He said, "Did God really say that you must not eat fruit from any tree in the garden?"

2The woman answered the snake, "We may eat fruit from the trees in the garden. 3But God told us, 'You must not eat fruit from the tree that is in the middle of the garden. You must not even touch it, or you will die.'"

⁴But the snake said to the woman, "You will not die. ⁵God knows that if you eat the fruit from that tree, you will learn about good and evil. Then you will be like God!"

⁶The woman saw that the tree was beautiful. She saw that its fruit was good to eat and that it would make her wise. So she took some of its fruit and ate it. She also gave some of the fruit to her husband, and he ate it.

⁷Then, it was as if the man's and the woman's eyes were opened. They realized they were naked. So they sewed fig leaves together and made something to cover themselves.

⁸Then they heard the Lord God walking in the garden. This was during the cool part of the day. And the man and his wife hid from the Lord God among the trees in the garden. ⁹But the Lord God called to the man. The Lord said, "Where are you?"

¹⁰The man answered, "I heard you walking in the garden. I was afraid because I was naked. So I hid."

¹¹God said to the man, "Who told you that you were naked? Did you eat fruit from that tree? I commanded you not to eat from that tree."

¹²The man said, "You gave this woman to me. She gave me fruit from the tree. So I ate it."

¹³Then the Lord God said to the woman, "What have you done?"

She answered, "The snake tricked me. So I ate the fruit."

¹⁴ªThe Lord God said to the snake,

> "Because you did this,
>> a curse will be put on you."

16a Then God said to the woman,

> "I will cause you to have much trouble . . .
>
> when you give birth to children."

17a Then God said to the man, "You listened to what your wife said. And you ate fruit from the tree that I commanded you not to eat from.

> "So I will put a curse on the ground.
>
> You will have to work very hard for food."

21The Lord God made clothes from animal skins for the man and his wife. And so the Lord dressed them. **22**Then the Lord God said, "Look, the man has become like one of us. He knows good and evil. And now we must keep him from eating some of the fruit from the tree of life. If he does, he will live forever." **23a**So the Lord God forced the man out of the garden of Eden.

Noah and the Flood

(From Genesis 6—9)

[6:9b] Noah was a good man. He was the most innocent man of his time. He walked with God. ¹⁰Noah had three sons: Shem, Ham and Japheth.

¹¹People on earth did what God said was evil. Violence was everywhere. ¹²And God saw this evil. All people on the earth did only evil. ¹³So God said to Noah, "People have made the earth full of violence. So I will destroy all people from the earth. ¹⁴Build a boat of cypress wood for yourself. Make rooms in it and cover it inside

and outside with tar. ¹⁷I will bring a flood of water on the earth. I will destroy all living things that live under the sky. This includes everything that has the breath of life. Everything on the earth will die. ¹⁸But I will make an agreement with you. You, your sons, your wife and your sons' wives will all go into the boat. ¹⁹Also, you must bring into the boat two of every living thing, male and female. Keep them alive with you.

²²Noah did everything that God commanded him.

[7:7] He and his wife and his sons and their wives went into the boat. They went in to escape the waters of the flood. ⁸The . . . animals . . . ^{9a}went into the boat. ¹⁰Seven days later the flood started.

¹²The rain fell on the earth for 40 days and 40 nights.

¹⁹The water rose so much that even the highest mountains under the sky were covered by it.

[22a] So everything on dry land died. [23b] All that was left was Noah and what was with him in the boat. [24] And the waters continued to cover the earth for 150 days.

[8:1a] But God remembered Noah and all the wild animals and tame animals with him in the boat. God made a wind blow over the earth. [3–4a] The water that covered the earth began to go down. After 150 days the water had gone down so much that the boat touched land again. It came to rest on one of the mountains of Ararat.

[8] Then Noah sent out a dove. This was to find out if the water had dried up from the ground. [9a] The dove could not find a place to land because water still covered the earth. So it came back to the boat.

[10] After seven days Noah again sent out the dove from the boat. [11a] And that evening it came back to him with a fresh olive leaf in

its mouth. ¹²Seven days later he sent the dove out again. But this time it did not come back.

¹⁵Then God said to Noah, ¹⁶"You and your wife, your sons and their wives should go out of the boat. ¹⁷ᵃBring every animal out of the boat with you."

[9:8] Then God said to Noah and his sons, ⁹"Now I am making my agreement with you and your people who will live after you. ¹⁰ᵃAnd I also make it with every living thing that is with you. ¹¹ᵇI will never again destroy all living things by floodwaters. A flood will never again destroy the earth.

¹³"I am putting my rainbow in the clouds. It is the sign of the agreement between me and the earth. ¹⁴When I bring clouds over the earth, a rainbow appears in the clouds. ¹⁵ᵃThen I will remember my agreement."

Joseph Sold into Slavery

(From Genesis 37)

[37:18] Joseph's brothers saw him coming from far away. Before he reached them, they made a plan to kill him. ¹⁹They said to each other, "Here comes that dreamer. ²⁰Let's kill him and throw his body into one of the wells. We can tell our father that a wild animal killed him. Then we will see what will become of his dreams."

²¹But Reuben heard their plan and saved Joseph. He said, "Let's not kill him. ²²Don't spill any blood. Throw him into this well here in the desert. But don't hurt him!" Reuben planned to save Joseph

later and send him back to his father. ²³So when Joseph came to his brothers, they pulled off his robe with long sleeves. ²⁴Then they threw him into the well. It was empty. There was no water in it.

²⁵While Joseph was in the well, the brothers sat down to eat. When they looked up, they saw a group of Ishmaelites. They were traveling from Gilead to Egypt. Their camels were carrying spices, balm and myrrh.

²⁶Then Judah said to his brothers, "What will we gain if we kill our brother and hide his death? ²⁷Let's sell him to these Ishmaelites. Then we will not be guilty of killing our own brother. . . ." And the other brothers agreed. ²⁸So when the Midianite traders came by, the brothers took Joseph out of the well. They sold him to the Ishmaelites for eight ounces of silver. And the Ishmaelites took him to Egypt.

²⁹Reuben was not with his brothers when they sold Joseph to the Ishmaelites. When Reuben came back to the well, Joseph was not there. Reuben tore his clothes to show he was sad. ³⁰Then he went back to his brothers and said, "The boy is not there! What will I do?" ³¹The brothers killed a goat and dipped Joseph's long-sleeved robe in its blood. ³²Then they brought the robe to their father. They said, "We found this robe. Look it over carefully. See if it is your son's robe."

[33]Jacob looked it over and said, "It is my son's robe! Some savage animal has eaten him. My son Joseph has been torn to pieces!" [34]Then Jacob tore his clothes and put on rough cloth to show that he was sad. He continued to be sad about his son for a long time. [35]All of Jacob's sons and daughters tried to comfort him. But he could not be comforted. Jacob said, "I will be sad about my son until the day I die." So Jacob cried for his son Joseph.

[36]Meanwhile the Midianites who had bought Joseph had taken him to Egypt. There they sold him to Potiphar. Potiphar was an officer to the king of Egypt and captain of the palace guard.

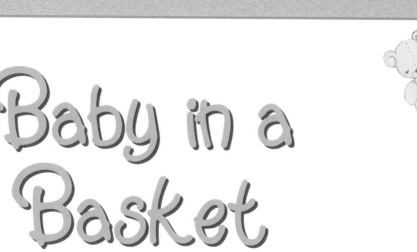

Baby in a Basket

(From Exodus 2)

[2:1] There was a man from the family of Levi. He married a woman who was also from the family of Levi. ²She became pregnant and gave birth to a son. She saw how wonderful the baby was, and she hid him for three months. ³But after three months, she was not able to hide the baby any longer. So she got a basket and covered it with tar so that it would float. She put the baby in the basket. Then she put the basket among the tall grass at the edge of the Nile River. ⁴The baby's sister stood a short distance away. She wanted to see what would happen to him.

⁵Then the daughter of the king of Egypt came to the river. She was going to take a bath. Her servant girls were walking beside the river. She saw the basket in the tall grass. So she sent her slave girl to get it. ⁶The king's daughter opened the basket and saw the baby boy. He was crying, and she felt sorry for him. She said, "This is one of the Hebrew babies."

⁷Then the baby's sister asked the king's daughter, "Would you like me to find a Hebrew woman to nurse the baby for you?"

⁸The king's daughter said, "Yes, please." So the girl went and got the baby's own mother.

⁹The king's daughter said to the woman, "Take this baby and nurse him for me. I will pay you." So the woman took her baby and nursed him. ¹⁰After the child had grown older, the woman took him to the king's daughter. She adopted the baby as her own

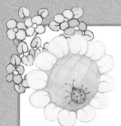

son. The king's daughter named him Moses, because she had pulled him out of the water.

[11]Moses grew and became a man. One day he visited his people, the Hebrews. He saw that they were forced to work very hard. He saw an Egyptian beating a Hebrew man, one of Moses' own people. [12]Moses looked all around and saw that no one was watching. So he killed the Egyptian and hid his body in the sand.

[13]The next day Moses returned and saw two Hebrew men fighting each other. He saw that one man was in the wrong. Moses said to that man, "Why are you hitting one of your own people?"

[14]The man answered, "Who made you our ruler and judge? Are you going to kill me as you killed the Egyptian?"

Then Moses was afraid. He thought, "Now everyone knows what I did."

¹⁵When the king heard about what Moses had done, he tried to kill Moses. But Moses ran away from the king and went to live in the land of Midian. There he sat down near a well.

Walls of Water

(From Exodus 14)

[14:5] The king of Egypt was told that the people of Israel had already left. Then he and his officers changed their minds about them. They said, "What have we done? We have let the people of Israel leave. We have lost our slaves!" 6So the king prepared his war chariot and took his army with him. 7He took 600 of his best chariots. He also took all the other chariots of Egypt. Each chariot had an officer in it. 8The Lord made the king of Egypt stubborn. So he chased the Israelites, who were leaving victoriously. 9bThey caught up with the Israelites while they were camped by the Red Sea. . . .

¹⁰The Israelites saw the king and his army coming after them. They were very frightened and cried to the Lord for help. ¹¹ᵃThey said to Moses, "What have you done to us? Why did you bring us out of Egypt to die in the desert?"

¹³But Moses answered, "Don't be afraid! Stand still and see the Lord save you today. You will never see these Egyptians again after today. ¹⁴You will only need to remain calm. The Lord will fight for you."

¹⁵Then the Lord said to Moses, "Why are you crying out to me? Command the people of Israel to start moving. ¹⁶Raise your walking stick and hold it over the sea. The sea will split. Then the people can cross the sea on dry land. ¹⁷I have made the Egyptians stubborn so they will chase the Israelites. But I will be honored when I defeat the king and all of his chariot drivers and chariots.

¹⁸I will defeat the king, his chariot drivers and chariots. Then Egypt will know that I am the Lord."

²¹Moses held his hand over the sea. All that night the Lord drove back the sea with a strong east wind. And so he made the sea become dry ground. The water was split. ²²And the Israelites went through the sea on dry land. A wall of water was on both sides.

²³Then all the king's horses, chariots and chariot drivers followed them into the sea. ²⁴Between two and six o'clock in the morning, the Lord looked down from the pillar of cloud and fire at the Egyptian army. He made them panic. ²⁵He kept the wheels of the chariots from turning. This made it hard to drive the chariots. The Egyptians shouted, "Let's get away from the Israelites! The Lord is fighting for them and against us Egyptians."

²⁶Then the Lord told Moses, "Hold your hand over the sea. Then the water will come back over the Egyptians, their chariots and chariot drivers." ²⁷So Moses raised his hand over the sea. And at dawn the water became deep again. The Egyptians were trying to run from it. But the Lord swept them away into the sea.

²⁹But the people of Israel crossed the sea on dry land. There was a wall of water on their right and on their left.

God's Commands

(From Exodus 19 and 20)

[19:1] Exactly three months after the Israelites had left Egypt, they reached the Desert of Sinai. ²They had left Rephidim and had come to the Desert of Sinai. The Israelites camped in the desert in front of Mount Sinai.

¹⁶ᵇThere was thunder and lightning with a thick cloud on the mountain. And there was a very loud blast from a trumpet. All the people in the camp were frightened. ¹⁷Then Moses led the people out of the camp to meet God. They stood at the foot of the mountain. ¹⁹ᵇThen Moses spoke, and the voice of God answered him.

[20:1] Then God spoke all these words:

²"I am the Lord your God. I brought you out of the land of Egypt where you were slaves.

³"You must not have any other gods except me.

⁴"You must not make for yourselves any idols. Don't make something that looks like anything in the sky above or on the earth below or in the water below the land.

⁷"You must not use the name of the Lord your God thoughtlessly. The Lord will punish anyone who is guilty and misuses his name.

⁸"Remember to keep the Sabbath as a holy day.

¹²ᵃ"Honor your father and your mother. Then you will live a long time in the land.

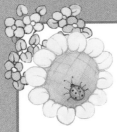

¹³"You must not murder anyone.

¹⁴"You must not be guilty of adultery.

¹⁵"You must not steal.

¹⁶"You must not tell lies about your neighbor in court.

¹⁷"You must not want to take your neighbor's house. . . . You must not want to take anything that belongs to your neighbor."

The People's Sin

(From Exodus 31 and 32)

[31:18] So the Lord finished speaking to Moses on Mount Sinai. Then the Lord gave him the two stone tablets with the agreement written on them. The finger of God wrote the commands on the stones.

[32:1] The people saw that a long time had passed. And Moses had not come down from the mountain. So they gathered around Aaron. They said to him, "Moses led us out of Egypt. But we don't know what has happened to him. So make us gods who will lead us."

²ᵃAaron said to the people, "Take off the gold earrings that your wives, sons and daughters are wearing." ⁴ᵃAaron took the gold from the people. Then he melted it and made a statue of a calf.

⁷And the Lord said to Moses, "Go down from this mountain. Your people, the people you brought out of the land of Egypt, have done a terrible sin."

¹⁵ᵃThen Moses went down the mountain. In his hands he had the two stone tablets with the agreement on them.

¹⁹When Moses came close to the camp, he saw the gold calf. . . . He became very angry. He threw down the stone tablets which he was carrying. He broke them at the bottom of the mountain.

³¹So Moses went back to the Lord and said, "How terrible it is! These people have sinned horribly. They have made for themselves gods from gold. ³²ᵃNow, forgive them of this sin."

David and Goliath

(From 1 Samuel 17)

[17:4] The Philistines had a champion fighter named Goliath. He was from Gath. He was about nine feet four inches tall. He came out of the Philistine camp.

8Goliath stood and shouted to the Israelite soldiers, "Why have you taken positions for battle? I am a Philistine, and you are Saul's servants! Choose a man and send him to fight me."

26David asked the men who stood near him, "What will be done to reward the man who kills this Philistine? . . . Why does [Goliath] think he can speak against the armies of the living God?"

³¹Some men heard what David said and told Saul. Then Saul ordered David to be sent to him.

³²David said to Saul, "Don't let anyone be discouraged. I, your servant, will go and fight this Philistine!

³⁷"The Lord saved me from a lion and a bear. He will also save me from this Philistine."

Saul said to David, "Go, and may the Lord be with you." ³⁸Saul put his own clothes on David. He put a bronze helmet on David's head and armor on his body. ³⁹David put on Saul's sword and tried to walk around. But he was not used to all the armor Saul had put on him.

He said to Saul, "I can't go in this. I'm not used to it." Then David took it all off. ⁴⁰He took his stick in his hand. And he chose five smooth stones from a stream. He put them in his pouch and held his sling in his hand. Then he went to meet Goliath.

41At the same time, the Philistine was coming closer to David. The man who held his shield walked in front of him. 42Goliath looked at David. He saw that David was only a boy, tanned and handsome. He looked down at David with disgust. 43He said, "Do you think I am a dog, that you come at me with a stick?" He used his gods' names to curse David. 44He said to David, "Come here. I'll feed your body to the birds of the air and the wild animals!"

45But David said to him, "You come to me using a sword, a large spear and a small spear. But I come to you in the name of the Lord of heaven's armies. He's the God of the armies of Israel! You have spoken out against him. 46Today the Lord will give you to me. . . . Then all the world will know there is a God in Israel! 47Everyone

gathered here will know the Lord does not need swords or spears to save people. The battle belongs to him! And he will help us defeat all of you."

48As Goliath came near to attack him, David ran quickly to meet him. 49He took a stone from his pouch. He put it into his sling and slung it. The stone hit the Philistine on his forehead and sank into it. Goliath fell facedown on the ground.

50So David defeated the Philistine with only a sling and a stone! He hit him and killed him. He did not even have a sword in his hand.

The Sermon on the Mount

(From Matthew 5)

[5:1] Jesus saw the crowds who were there. He went up on a hill and sat down. His followers came to him. ²Jesus taught the people and said:

> ³"Those people who know they have great spiritual needs
>
> are happy.
>
> The kingdom of heaven belongs to them.
>
> ⁴Those who are sad now are happy.
>
> God will comfort them.

⁵Those who are humble are happy.

The earth will belong to them.

⁶Those who want to do right more than anything else are

happy.

God will fully satisfy them.

⁷Those who give mercy to others are happy.

Mercy will be given to them.

⁸Those who are pure in their thinking are happy.

They will be with God.

⁹Those who work to bring peace are happy.

God will call them his sons.

¹⁰Those who are treated badly for doing good are happy.

The kingdom of heaven belongs to them.

¹¹"People will say bad things about you and hurt you. They will lie and say all kinds of evil things about you because you follow me.

But when they do these things to you, you are happy. [12]Rejoice and be glad. You have a great reward waiting for you in heaven. People did the same evil things to the prophets who lived before you.

[13]"You are the salt of the earth. But if the salt loses its salty taste, it cannot be made salty again. It is good for nothing. It must be thrown out for people to walk on.

[14]"You are the light that gives light to the world. A city that is built on a hill cannot be hidden. [15]And people don't hide a light under a bowl. They put the light on a lampstand. Then the light shines for all the people in the house. [16]In the same way, you should be a light for other people. Live so that they will see the good things you do. Live so that they will praise your Father in heaven.

[38]"You have heard that it was said, 'An eye for an eye, and a tooth for a tooth.' [39]But I tell you, don't stand up against an evil person.

If someone slaps you on the right cheek, then turn and let him slap the other cheek too. ⁴⁰If someone wants to sue you in court and take your shirt, then let him have your coat too. ⁴¹If a soldier forces you to go with him one mile, then go with him two miles. ⁴²If a person asks you for something, then give it to him. Don't refuse to give to a person who wants to borrow from you.

⁴³"You have heard that it was said, 'Love your neighbor and hate your enemies.' ⁴⁴But I tell you, love your enemies. Pray for those who hurt you. ⁴⁵ªIf you do this, then you will be true sons of your Father in heaven."

Jesus Feeds More Than 5,000 People and Walks on Water

(From Matthew 14)

[14:13b] Jesus left in a boat. He went to a lonely place by himself. But when the crowds heard about it, they followed him on foot from the towns. 14When Jesus arrived, he saw a large crowd. He felt sorry for them and healed those who were sick.

¹⁵Late that afternoon, his followers came to Jesus and said, "No one lives in this place. And it is already late. Send the people away so they can go to the towns and buy food for themselves."

¹⁶Jesus answered, "They don't need to go away. You give them some food to eat."

¹⁷The followers answered, "But we have only five loaves of bread and two fish."

¹⁸Jesus said, "Bring the bread and the fish to me." ¹⁹Then he told the people to sit down on the grass. He took the five loaves of bread and the two fish. Then he looked to heaven and thanked God for the food. Jesus divided the loaves of bread. He gave them to his followers, and they gave the bread to the people. ²⁰All the people ate and were satisfied. After they finished eating, the

followers filled 12 baskets with the pieces of food that were not eaten. ²¹There were about 5,000 men there who ate, as well as women and children.

²²Then Jesus made his followers get into the boat. He told them to go ahead of him to the other side of the lake. Jesus stayed there to tell the people they could go home. ²³After he said good-bye to them, he went alone up into the hills to pray. It was late, and Jesus was there alone. ²⁴By this time, the boat was already far away on the lake. The boat was having trouble because of the waves, and the wind was blowing against it.

²⁵Between three and six o'clock in the morning, Jesus' followers were still in the boat. Jesus came to them. He was walking on the water. ²⁶When the followers saw him walking on the water, they were afraid. They said, "It's a ghost!" and cried out in fear.

²⁷But Jesus quickly spoke to them. He said, "Have courage! It is I! Don't be afraid."

²⁸Peter said, "Lord, if that is really you, then tell me to come to you on the water."

²⁹Jesus said, "Come."

And Peter left the boat and walked on the water to Jesus. ³⁰But when Peter saw the wind and the waves, he became afraid and began to sink. He shouted, "Lord, save me!"

³¹Then Jesus reached out his hand and caught Peter. Jesus said, "Your faith is small. Why did you doubt?"

³²After Peter and Jesus were in the boat, the wind became calm. ³³Then those who were in the boat worshiped Jesus and said, "Truly you are the Son of God!"

Jesus Rides into Jerusalem on a Donkey

(From Matthew 21)

[21:1] Jesus and his followers were coming closer to Jerusalem. But first they stopped at Bethphage at the hill called the Mount of Olives. From there Jesus sent two of his followers into the town. ²He said to them, "Go to the town you can see there. When you enter it, you will find a donkey tied there with its colt. Untie them and bring them to me. ³If anyone asks you why you are taking the

donkeys, tell him, 'The Master needs them. He will send them back soon.' "

⁴This was to make clear the full meaning of what the prophet said:

⁵"Tell the people of Jerusalem,

'Your king is coming to you.

He is gentle and riding on a donkey.

He is on the colt of a donkey.' "

⁶The followers went and did what Jesus told them to do. ⁷They brought the donkey and the colt to Jesus. They laid their coats on the donkeys, and Jesus sat on them. ⁸Many people spread their coats on the road before Jesus. Others cut branches from the trees and spread them on the road. ⁹Some of the people were walking ahead of Jesus. Others were walking behind him. All the people were shouting,

"Praise to the Son of David!

God bless the One who comes in the name of the Lord!

Praise to God in heaven!"

[10]Then Jesus went into Jerusalem. The city was filled with excitement. The people asked, "Who is this man?"

[11]The crowd answered, "This man is Jesus. He is the prophet from the town of Nazareth in Galilee."

The Last Supper

(From Mark 14)

[14:12] It was now the first day of the Feast of Unleavened Bread. This was a time when the Jews always sacrificed the Passover lambs. Jesus' followers came to him. They said, "We will go and prepare everything for the Passover Feast. Where do you want to eat the feast?"

13Jesus sent two of his followers and said to them, "Go into the city. A man carrying a jar of water will meet you. Follow him. 14He will go into a house. Tell the owner of the house, 'The Teacher asks that

you show us the room where he and his followers can eat the Passover Feast.' ¹⁵The owner will show you a large room upstairs. This room is ready. Prepare the food for us there."

¹⁶So the followers left and went into the city. Everything happened as Jesus had said. So they prepared the Passover Feast.

¹⁷In the evening, Jesus went to that house with the 12.

²²While they were eating, Jesus took some bread. He thanked God for it and broke it. Then he gave it to his followers and said, "Take it. This bread is my body."

²³Then Jesus took a cup. He thanked God for it and gave it to the followers. All the followers drank from the cup.

²⁴Then Jesus said, "This is my blood which begins the new agreement that God makes with his people. This blood is poured out for

many. ²⁵I tell you the truth. I will not drink of this fruit of the vine again until that day when I drink it new in the kingdom of God."

²⁶They sang a hymn and went out to the Mount of Olives.

Jesus Is Born

(From Luke 2)

[2:1] At that time, Augustus Caesar sent an order to all people in the countries that were under Roman rule. The order said that they must list their names in a register. ²This was the first registration taken while Quirinius was governor of Syria. ³And everyone went to their own towns to be registered.

⁴So Joseph left Nazareth, a town in Galilee. He went to the town of Bethlehem in Judea. This town was known as the town of David. Joseph went there because he was from the family of David.

⁵Joseph registered with Mary because she was engaged to marry him. (Mary was now pregnant.) ⁶While Joseph and Mary were in Bethlehem, the time came for her to have the baby. ⁷She gave birth to her first son. There were no rooms left in the inn. So she wrapped the baby with cloths and laid him in a box where animals are fed.

⁸That night, some shepherds were in the fields nearby watching their sheep. ⁹An angel of the Lord stood before them. The glory of the Lord was shining around them, and suddenly they became very frightened. ¹⁰The angel said to them, "Don't be afraid, because I am bringing you some good news. It will be a joy to all the people. ¹¹Today your Savior was born in David's town. He is Christ, the Lord. ¹²This is how you will know him: You will find a baby wrapped in cloths and lying in a feeding box."

¹³Then a very large group of angels from heaven joined the first angel. All the angels were praising God, saying:

> ¹⁴"Give glory to God in heaven,
>
>> and on earth let there be peace to the people who
>>
>> please God."

¹⁵Then the angels left the shepherds and went back to heaven. The shepherds said to each other, "Let us go to Bethlehem and see this thing that has happened. We will see this thing the Lord told us about."

¹⁶So the shepherds went quickly and found Mary and Joseph. ¹⁷And the shepherds saw the baby lying in a feeding box. Then they told what the angels had said about this child. ¹⁸Everyone was amazed when they heard what the shepherds said to them. ¹⁹Mary hid these things in her heart; she continued to think about

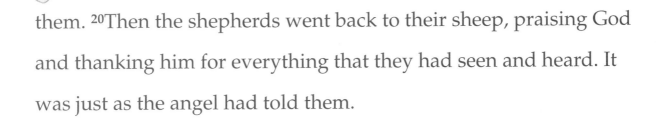

them. ²⁰Then the shepherds went back to their sheep, praising God and thanking him for everything that they had seen and heard. It was just as the angel had told them.

²²The time came for Mary and Joseph to do what the law of Moses taught about being made pure. They took Jesus to Jerusalem to present him to the Lord. ²³It is written in the law of the Lord: "Give every firstborn male to the Lord." ²⁴Mary and Joseph also went to offer a sacrifice, as the law of the Lord says: "You must sacrifice two doves or two young pigeons."

Jesus Visits the Temple with His Parents

(From Luke 2)

[2:39] Joseph and Mary . . . went home to Nazareth, their own town in Galilee. ⁴⁰The little child began to grow up. He became stronger and wiser, and God's blessings were with him.

⁴¹Every year Jesus' parents went to Jerusalem for the Passover Feast. ⁴²When Jesus was 12 years old, they went to the feast as they always did. ⁴³When the feast days were over, they went home. The

boy Jesus stayed behind in Jerusalem, but his parents did not know it. ⁴⁴Joseph and Mary traveled for a whole day. They thought that Jesus was with them in the group. Then they began to look for him among their family and friends, ⁴⁵but they did not find him. So they went back to Jerusalem to look for him there. ⁴⁶After three days they found him. Jesus was sitting in the Temple with the religious teachers, listening to them and asking them questions. ⁴⁷All who heard him were amazed at his understanding and wise answers. ⁴⁸When Jesus' parents saw him, they were amazed. His mother said to him, "Son, why did you do this to us? Your father and I were very worried about you. We have been looking for you."

⁴⁹Jesus asked, "Why did you have to look for me? You should have known that I must be where my Father's work is!" ⁵⁰But they did not understand the meaning of what he said.

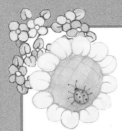

⁵¹ᵃJesus went with them to Nazareth and obeyed them. ⁵²Jesus continued to learn more and more and to grow physically. People liked him, and he pleased God

Jesus Goes Back to Heaven

(From Luke 24)

[24:36] While the two followers were telling this, Jesus himself stood among those gathered. He said to them, "Peace be with you."

³⁷They were fearful and terrified. They thought they were seeing a ghost. ³⁸But Jesus said, "Why are you troubled? Why do you doubt what you see? ³⁹Look at my hands and my feet. It is I myself!

Touch me. You can see that I have a living body; a ghost does not have a body like this."

⁴⁰After Jesus said this, he showed them his hands and feet. ⁴¹The followers were amazed and very happy. They still could not believe it. Jesus said to them, "Do you have any food here?" ⁴²They gave him a piece of cooked fish. ⁴³While the followers watched, Jesus took the fish and ate it.

⁴⁴He said to them, "Remember when I was with you before? I said that everything written about me must happen—everything in the law of Moses, the books of the prophets, and the Psalms."

⁴⁵Then Jesus opened their minds so they could understand the Scriptures. ⁴⁶He said to them, "It is written that the Christ would be killed and rise from death on the third day. ⁴⁷⁻⁴⁸You saw these

things happen—you are witnesses. You must tell people to change their hearts and lives. If they do this, their sins will be forgiven. You must start at Jerusalem and preach these things in my name to all nations. [49]Listen! My Father has promised you something; I will send it to you. But you must stay in Jerusalem until you have received that power from heaven."

[50]Jesus led his followers out of Jerusalem almost to Bethany. He raised his hands and blessed them. [51]While he was blessing them, he was separated from them and carried into heaven. [52]They worshiped him and then went back to the city very happy. [53]They stayed in the Temple all the time, praising God.

The Empty Tomb

(From John 19 and 20)

[19:38] Later, a man named Joseph from Arimathea asked Pilate if he could take the body of Jesus. (Joseph was a secret follower of Jesus, because he was afraid of the Jews.) Pilate gave his permission. So Joseph came and took Jesus' body away. 39Nicodemus went with Joseph. Nicodemus was the man who earlier had come to Jesus at night. He brought about 75 pounds of spices. This was a mixture of myrrh and aloes. 40These two men took Jesus' body and wrapped it with the spices in pieces of linen cloth. (This is how the Jews bury people.) 41In the place where Jesus was killed, there was

a garden. In the garden was a new tomb where no one had ever been buried. [42]The men laid Jesus in that tomb because it was near, and the Jews were preparing to start their Sabbath day.

[20:1] Early on the first day of the week, Mary Magdalene went to the tomb. It was still dark. Mary saw that the large stone had been moved away from the tomb. [2]So Mary ran to Simon Peter and the other follower (the one Jesus loved). Mary said, "They have taken the Lord out of the tomb. We don't know where they have put him."

[3]So Peter and the other follower started for the tomb. [4]They were both running, but the other follower ran faster than Peter. So the other follower reached the tomb first. [5]He bent down and looked in. He saw the strips of linen cloth lying there, but he did not go in. [6]Then following him came Simon Peter. He went into the tomb

and saw the strips of linen lying there. [7]He also saw the cloth that had been around Jesus' head. The cloth was folded up and laid in a different place from the strips of linen. [8]Then the other follower, who had reached the tomb first, also went in. He saw and believed. [9](These followers did not yet understand from the Scriptures that Jesus must rise from death.)

[10]Then the followers went back home. [11]But Mary stood outside the tomb, crying. While she was still crying, she bent down and looked inside the tomb. [12]She saw two angels dressed in white. They were sitting where Jesus' body had been, one at the head and one at the feet.

[13]They asked her, "Woman, why are you crying?"

She answered, "They have taken away my Lord. I don't know where they have put him." [14]When Mary said this, she turned

around and saw Jesus standing there. But she did not know that it was Jesus.

¹⁵Jesus asked her, "Woman, why are you crying? Whom are you looking for?"

Mary thought he was the gardener. So she said to him, "Did you take him away, sir? Tell me where you put him, and I will get him."

¹⁶Jesus said to her, "Mary."

Mary turned toward Jesus and said in the Jewish language, "Rabboni." (This means Teacher.)

¹⁷Jesus said to her, "Don't hold me. I have not yet gone up to the Father. But go to my brothers and tell them this: 'I am going back

to my Father and your Father. I am going back to my God and your God.' "

18Mary Magdalene went and said to the followers, "I saw the Lord!" And she told them what Jesus had said to her.

Jesus Appears to His Followers

(From John 20 and 21)

[20:19] It was the first day of the week. That evening the followers were together. The doors were locked, because they were afraid of the Jews. Then Jesus came and stood among them. He said, "Peace be with you!" [20]After he said this, he showed them his hands and his side. The followers were very happy when they saw the Lord.

21Then Jesus said again, "Peace be with you! As the Father sent me, I now send you." 22After he said this, he breathed on them and said, "Receive the Holy Spirit. 23If you forgive anyone his sins, they are forgiven. If you don't forgive them, they are not forgiven."

24Thomas . . . was not with the followers when Jesus came. Thomas was 1 of the 12. 25The other followers told Thomas, "We saw the Lord."

But Thomas said, "I will not believe it until I see the nail marks in his hands. And I will not believe until I put my finger where the nails were and put my hand into his side."

26A week later the followers were in the house again. Thomas was with them. The doors were locked, but Jesus came in and stood among them. He said, "Peace be with you!" 27Then he said to

Thomas, "Put your finger here. Look at my hands. Put your hand here in my side. Stop doubting and believe."

28Thomas said to him, "My Lord and my God!"

29Then Jesus told him, "You believe because you see me. Those who believe without seeing me will be truly happy."

[21:1a] Later, Jesus showed himself to his followers by Lake Galilee. 2aSome of the followers were together. 3Simon Peter said, "I am going out to fish."

The other followers said, "We will go with you." So they went out and got into the boat. They fished that night but caught nothing.

4Early the next morning Jesus stood on the shore. But the followers did not know that it was Jesus. 5Then he said to them, "Friends, have you caught any fish?"

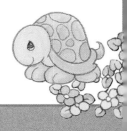

They answered, "No."

[6]He said, "Throw your net into the water on the right side of the boat, and you will find some." So they did this. They caught so many fish that they could not pull the net back into the boat.

[7]The follower whom Jesus loved said to Peter, "It is the Lord!" When Peter heard him say this, he wrapped his coat around himself. (Peter had taken his clothes off.) Then he jumped into the water. [8a]The other followers went to shore in the boat, dragging the net full of fish. [9]When the followers stepped out of the boat and onto the shore, they saw a fire of hot coals. There were fish on the fire, and there was bread.

[12]Jesus said to them, "Come and eat." None of the followers dared ask him, "Who are you?" They knew it was the Lord. [13]Jesus came and took the bread and gave it to them. He also gave them the fish.

Words of Praise and Wisdom

Your Name Is Wonderful

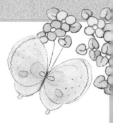

(From Psalm 8)

¹Lord our Master,

　　your name is the most wonderful name in all

　　the earth!

　　It brings you praise in heaven above.

²You have taught children and babies

　　to sing praises to you.

　　This is because of your enemies.

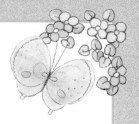

And so you silence your enemies

and destroy those who try to get even.

³I look at the heavens,

which you made with your hands.

I see the moon and stars,

which you created.

⁴But why is man important to you?

Why do you take care of human beings?

⁵You made man a little lower than the angels.

And you crowned him with glory and honor.

⁶You put him in charge of everything you made.

You put all things under his control:

⁷all the sheep, the cattle

   and the wild animals,

⁸the birds in the sky,

   the fish in the sea,

   and everything that lives under water.

⁹Lord our Master,

   your name is the most wonderful name in all

   the earth!

The Lord Takes Care of His People

(From Psalm 16)

¹Protect me, God,

because I trust in you.

²I said to the Lord, "You are my Lord.

Every good thing I have comes from you."

³There are godly people in the world.

I enjoy them.

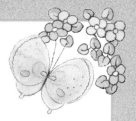

⁵No, the Lord is all need.

   He takes care of me.

⁶My share in life has been pleasant.

   My part has been beautiful.

⁷I praise the Lord because he guides me.

   Even at night, I feel his leading.

⁸I keep the Lord before me always.

   Because he is close by my side

   I will not be hurt.

⁹So I rejoice, and I am glad.

   Even my body has hope.

[11]You will teach me God's way to live.

Being with you will fill me with joy.

At your right hand I will find pleasure

forever.

The Lord Is My Shepherd

(From Psalm 23)

A song of David.

¹The Lord is my shepherd.

I have everything I need.

²He gives me rest in green pastures.

He leads me to calm water.

³   He gives me new strength.

For the good of his name,

he leads me on paths that are right.

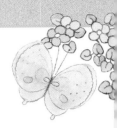

⁴Even if I walk

      through a very dark valley,

I will not be afraid

      because you are with me.

Your rod and your walking stick comfort me.

⁵You prepare a meal for me

      in front of my enemies.

You pour oil on my head.

      You give me more than I can hold.

⁶Surely your goodness and love will be with me

      all my life.

And I will live in the house of the Lord forever.

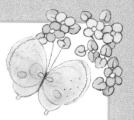

Tell the Truth

(From Psalm 32)

¹Happy is the person

　　whose sins are forgiven,

　　whose wrongs are pardoned.

²Happy is the person

　　whom the Lord does not consider guilty.

　　In that person there is nothing false.

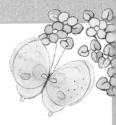

³When I kept things to myself,

I felt weak deep inside me.

I moaned all day long.

⁴Day and night

you punished me.

My strength was gone

as in the summer heat.

⁵Then I confessed my sins to you.

I didn't hide my guilt.

I said, "I will confess my sins to the Lord."

And you forgave my guilt.

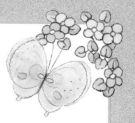

⁶For this reason, all who obey you

should pray to you while they still can.

When troubles rise like a flood,

they will not reach them.

⁷You are my hiding place.

You protect me from my troubles.

You fill me with songs of salvation.

⁸The Lord says, "I will make you wise. I will show

you where to go.

I will guide you and watch over you.

⁹So don't be like a horse or donkey.

They don't understand.

They must be led with bits and reins,

or they will not come near you."

[10]Wicked people have many troubles.

But the Lord's love surrounds those who

trust him.

[11]Good people, rejoice and be happy in the Lord.

All you whose hearts are right, sing.

Wishing to Be Near God

(From Psalm 63)

¹God, you are my God.

I want to follow you.

My whole being

thirsts for you,

like a man in a dry, empty land

where there is no water.

²I have seen you in the Temple.

I have seen your strength and glory.

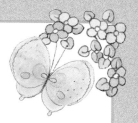

³Your love is better than life.

I will praise you.

⁴I will praise you as long as I live.

I will lift up my hands in prayer to your name.

⁵I will be content as if I had eaten the best foods.

My lips will sing. My mouth will praise you.

⁶I remember you while I'm lying in bed.

I think about you through the night.

⁷You are my help.

Because of your protection, I sing.

⁸I stay close to you.

You support me with your right hand.

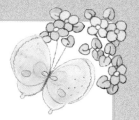

Lord, Teach Me Your Rules

(From Psalm 119)

¹Happy are the people who live pure lives.

They follow the Lord's teachings.

²Happy are the people who keep his rules.

They ask him for help with their whole heart.

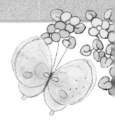

³They don't do what is wrong.

They follow his ways.

⁴Lord, you gave your orders

to be followed completely.

⁵I wish I were more loyal

in meeting your demands.

⁶Then I would not be ashamed

when I think of your commands.

⁷When I learned that your laws are fair,

I praised you with an honest heart.

⁸I will meet your demands.

So please don't ever leave me.

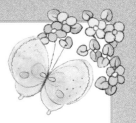

⁹How can a young person live a pure life?

He can do it by obeying your word.

¹⁰With all my heart I try to obey you, God.

Don't let me break your commands.

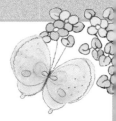

¹¹I have taken your words to heart

so I would not sin against you.

¹²Lord, you should be praised.

Teach me your demands.

¹³My lips will tell about

all the laws you have spoken.

¹⁴I enjoy living by your rules

as people enjoy great riches.

¹⁵I think about your orders

and study your ways.

¹⁶I enjoy obeying your demands.

And I will not forget your word.

[20]I want to study

    your laws all the time.

[24]Your rules give me pleasure.

    They give me good advice.

The Word of God

(From Psalm 119)

⁷³You made me and formed me with your hands.

Give me understanding so I can learn your

commands.

⁷⁶Comfort me with your love,

as you promised me, your servant.

⁷⁷Have mercy on me so that I may live.

I love your teachings.

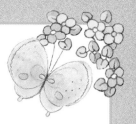

89Lord, your word is everlasting.

It continues forever in heaven.

90Your loyalty will continue from now on.

You made the earth, and it still stands.

105 Your word is like a lamp for my feet

and a light for my way.

111I will follow your rules forever.

They make me happy.

112I will try to do what you demand

forever, until the end.

114 You are my hiding place and my shield.

I trust your word.

[117]Help me, and I will be saved.

I will always respect your demands.

[127]I love your commands

more than the purest gold.

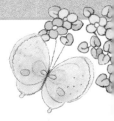

Protection and Guidance

(From Psalm 121)

¹I look up to the hills.

But where does my help come from?

²My help comes from the Lord.

He made heaven and earth.

³He will not let you be defeated.

He who guards you never sleeps.

⁴He who guards Israel

never rests or sleeps.

⁵The Lord guards you.

The Lord protects you as the shade protects

you from the sun.

⁶The sun cannot hurt you during the day.

And the moon cannot hurt you at night.

⁷The Lord will guard you from all dangers.

He will guard your life.

⁸The Lord will guard you as you come and go,

both now and forever.

Praise!

(From Psalm 150)

¹Praise the Lord!

Praise God in his Temple.

Praise him in his mighty heaven.

²Praise him for his strength.

Praise him for his greatness.

³Praise him with trumpet blasts.

Praise him with harps and lyres.

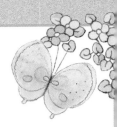

⁴Praise him with tambourines and dancing.

Praise him with stringed instruments and flutes.

⁵Praise him with loud cymbals.

Praise him with crashing cymbals.

⁶Let everything that breathes praise the Lord.

Praise the Lord!

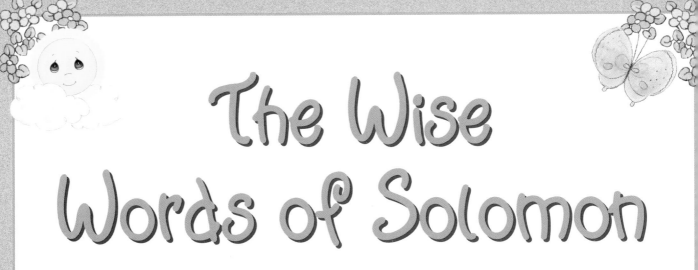

The Wise Words of Solomon

(From Proverbs 1)

¹These are the wise words of Solomon son of

David. Solomon was king of Israel.

²They teach wisdom and self-control.

They give understanding.

³They will teach you how to be wise and

self-controlled.

They will teach you what is honest and fair

and right.

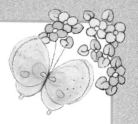

⁴They give the ability to think to those with little knowledge.

They give knowledge and good sense to the young.

⁵Wise people should also listen to them and learn even more.

Even smart people will find wise advice in these words.

⁶Then they will be able to understand wise words and stories.

They will understand the words of wise men and their riddles.

⁷Knowledge begins with respect for the Lord.

But foolish people hate wisdom and

self-control.

⁸My child, listen to your father's teaching.

And do not forget your mother's advice.

⁹Their teaching will beautify your life.

It will be like flowers in your hair or a chain

around your neck.

¹⁰My child, sinners will try to lead you into sin.

But do not follow them.

¹⁵My child, do not go along with them.

Do not do what they do.

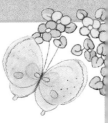

Rewards of Wisdom

(From Proverbs 2)

¹My child, believe what I say.

And remember what I command you.

²Listen to wisdom.

Try with all your heart to gain

understanding.

³Cry out for wisdom.

Beg for understanding.

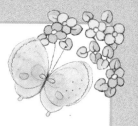

⁴Search for it as you would for silver.

Hunt for it like hidden treasure.

⁵Then you will understand what it means to

respect the Lord.

Then you will begin to know God.

⁶Only the Lord gives wisdom.

Knowledge and understanding come from

him.

⁷He stores up wisdom for those who are honest.

Like a shield he protects those who are

innocent.

⁸He guards those who are fair to others.

He protects those who are loyal to him.

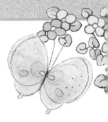

⁹Then you will understand what is honest and fair

and right.

You will understand what is good to do.

¹⁰You will have wisdom in your heart.

And knowledge will be pleasing to you.

¹¹Good sense will protect you.

Understanding will guard you.

¹²It will keep you from doing evil.

It will save you from people whose words

are bad.

Remember the Lord

(From Proverbs 3)

¹My child, do not forget my teaching.

Keep my commands in mind.

²Then you will live a long time.

And your life will be successful.

³Don't ever stop being kind and truthful.

Let kindness and truth show in all you do.

Write them down in your mind as if on

a tablet.

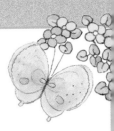

⁴Then you will be respected

and pleasing to both God and men.

⁵Trust the Lord with all your heart.

Don't depend on your own understanding.

⁶Remember the Lord in everything you do.

And he will give you success.

⁷Don't depend on your own wisdom.

Respect the Lord and refuse to do wrong.

⁸Then your body will be healthy.

And your bones will be strong.

Train Up a Child

(From Proverbs 22)

¹Being respected is more important than having

great riches.

To be well thought of is better than owning

silver or gold.

²The rich and the poor are alike

in that the Lord made them all.

³When a wise person sees danger ahead, he

avoids it.

But a foolish person keeps going and gets

into trouble.

⁴Respecting the Lord and not being proud

will bring you wealth, honor and life.

⁵The lives of evil people are like paths covered

with thorns and traps.

People who protect themselves don't have

such problems.

God
Bless our
Happy
Home

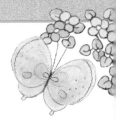

[6]Train a child how to live the right way.

Then even when he is old, he will still live

that way.

A Time to Laugh, a Time to Dance

(From Ecclesiastes 3)

¹There is a right time for everything.

Everything on earth has its special season.

²There is a time to be born

and a time to die.

There is a time to plant

and a time to pull up plants.

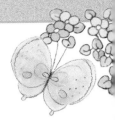

[3]There is a time to kill

and a time to heal.

There is a time to destroy

and a time to build.

[4]There is a time to cry

and a time to laugh.

There is a time to be sad

and a time to dance.

[5]There is a time to throw away stones

and a time to gather them.

There is a time to hug

and a time not to hug.

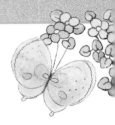

6There is a time to look for something

and a time to stop looking for it.

There is a time to keep things

and a time to throw things away.

7There is a time to tear apart

and a time to sew together.

There is a time to be silent

and a time to speak.

8There is a time to love

and a time to hate.

There is a time for war

and a time for peace.

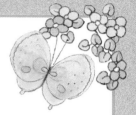

friends and family Give Strength

(From Ecclesiastes 4)

[9]Two people are better than one.

They get more done by working together.

[10]If one person falls,

the other can help him up.

But it is bad for the person who is alone when he

falls.

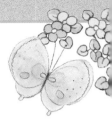

No one is there to help him.

¹¹If two lie down together, they will be warm.

But a person alone will not be warm.

¹²An enemy might defeat one person,

but two people together can defend

themselves.

A rope that has three parts wrapped together

is hard to break.

The King of Peace Is Coming

(From Isaiah 11)

¹A branch will grow

from a stump of a tree that was cut down.

So a new king will come

from the family of Jesse.

²The Spirit of the Lord will rest upon that king.

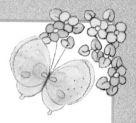

The Spirit gives him wisdom, understanding,

guidance and power.

And the Spirit teaches him to know and

respect the Lord.

³This king will be glad to obey the Lord.

He will not judge by the way things look.

He will not judge by what people say.

⁴He will judge the poor honestly.

He will be fair in his decisions for the poor

people of the land.

At his command evil people will be punished.

By his words the wicked will be put to death.

⁵Goodness and fairness will give him strength.

They will be like a belt around his waist.

⁶Then wolves will live in peace with lambs.

And leopards will lie down to rest with goats.

Calves, lions and young bulls will eat together.

And a little child will lead them.

⁷Cows and bears will eat together in peace.

Their young will lie down together.

Lions will eat hay as oxen do.

⁹They will not hurt or destroy each other

on all my holy mountain.

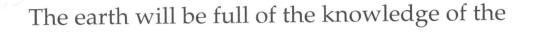

The earth will be full of the knowledge of the

Lord,

as the sea is full of water.

¹⁰At that time the new king from the family of Jesse will stand as a banner for the people. The nations will come together around him. And the place where he lives will be filled with glory.

More Stories of the Faith

We Will Serve the Lord!

(From Joshua 24)

[24:1a] Then all the tribes of Israel met together at Shechem.

²Then Joshua spoke to all the people. He said, "Here's what the Lord, the God of Israel, says to you: 'A long time ago your ancestors lived on the other side of the Euphrates River. . . . They worshiped other gods. ³But I, the Lord, took your ancestor Abraham out of the land on the other side of the river. I led him through the land of Canaan. And I gave him many children. I gave him his son Isaac. ⁴And I gave Isaac two sons named Jacob and Esau. I gave

the land around the mountains of Edom to Esau. But Jacob and his sons went down to Egypt. ⁵Then I sent Moses and Aaron to Egypt. I caused many terrible things to happen to the Egyptians. Then I brought you people out. ⁶When I brought your fathers out of Egypt, they came to the Red Sea. And the Egyptians chased them. There were chariots and men on horses. ⁷So the people asked me, the Lord, for help. And I caused great trouble to come to the Egyptians. I caused the sea to cover them. You yourselves saw what I did to the army of Egypt. After that, you lived in the desert for a long time.

⁸" 'Then I brought you to the land of the Amorites. This was east of the Jordan River. They fought against you, but I gave you the power to defeat them. I destroyed them before you. Then you took control of that land. ⁹But the king of Moab, Balak son of Zippor,

prepared to fight against the Israelites. The king sent for Balaam son of Beor to curse you. ¹⁰But I, the Lord, refused to listen to Balaam. So he asked for good things to happen to you! He blessed you many times. I saved you and brought you out of his power.

¹¹" 'Then you traveled across the Jordan River and came to Jericho. The people in the city of Jericho fought against you. . . . But I allowed you to defeat them all. ¹³ᵃIt was I, the Lord, who gave you that land. I gave you land where you did not have to work. I gave you cities that you did not have to build. And now you live in that land and in those cities.' "

¹⁴Then Joshua spoke to the people. He said, "Now you have heard the Lord's words. So you must respect the Lord and serve him fully and sincerely. Throw away the false gods that your people worshiped. . . . Now you must serve the Lord. ¹⁵But maybe you

don't want to serve the Lord. You must choose for yourselves today. You must decide whom you will serve. You may serve the gods that your people worshiped when they lived on the other side of the Euphrates River. Or you may serve the gods of the Amorites who lived in this land. As for me and my family, we will serve the Lord."

Daniel and the Lions' Den

(From Daniel 6)

[6:4a] So the other supervisors and the governors tried to find reasons to accuse Daniel. But he went on doing the business of the government. And they could not find anything wrong with him. So they could not accuse him of doing anything wrong.

[6]So the supervisors and the governors went as a group to the king. They said: "King Darius, live forever! [7b]We think the king should make this law that everyone would have to obey: No one should pray to any god or man except to you, our king. . . . Anyone who

doesn't obey will be thrown into the lions' den. 8aNow, our king, make the law. Write it down so it cannot be changed. . . ." 9So King Darius made the law and had it written.

10When Daniel heard that the new law had been written, he went to his house. He went to his upstairs room. The windows of that room opened toward Jerusalem. Three times each day Daniel got down on his knees and prayed. He prayed and thanked God, just as he always had done.

11Then those men went as a group and found Daniel. They saw him praying and asking God for help. 12So they went to the king. . . . They said, "Didn't you write a law that says no one may pray to any god or man except you, our king? Doesn't it say that anyone who disobeys . . . will be thrown into the lions' den?"

The king answered, "Yes, I wrote that law. And the laws of the Medes and Persians cannot be canceled."

¹³Then those men spoke to the king. They said, "Daniel is . . . not paying attention to the law you wrote. Daniel still prays to his God three times every day." ¹⁴ᵃThe king became very upset when he heard this.

¹⁵Then those men went as a group to the king. They said, "Remember, our king, the law of the Medes and Persians. It says that no law or command given by the king can be changed."

¹⁶So King Darius gave the order. They brought Daniel and threw him into the lions' den. The king said to Daniel, "May the God you serve all the time save you!" ¹⁷ᵃA big stone was brought. It was put over the opening of the lions' den. ¹⁸Then King Darius went back

to his palace. He did not eat that night. . . . And he could not sleep.

[19]The next morning King Darius got up at dawn. He hurried to the lions' den. [20]As he came near the den, he was worried. He called out to Daniel. He said, "Daniel, servant of the living God! Has your God that you always worship been able to save you from the lions?"

[21]Daniel answered, "My king, live forever! [22]My God sent his angel to close the lions' mouths. They have not hurt me, because my God knows I am innocent. I never did anything wrong to you, my king."

[23]King Darius was very happy. He told his servants to lift Daniel out of the lions' den. So they lifted him out and did not find any injury on him. This was because Daniel had trusted in his God.

Jonah Runs from God

(From Jonah 1 and 2)

[1:1] The Lord spoke his word to Jonah son of Amittai: ²"Get up, go to the great city of Nineveh and preach against it. I see the evil things they do."

³But Jonah got up to run away from the Lord. He went to the city of Joppa. There he found a ship that was going to the city of Tarshish. Jonah paid for the trip and went aboard. He wanted to go to Tarshish to run away from the Lord.

4But the Lord sent a great wind on the sea. This wind made the sea very rough. So the ship was in danger of breaking apart. 5The sailors were afraid. Each man cried to his own god. The men began throwing the cargo into the sea. This would make the ship lighter so it would not sink.

But Jonah had gone down into the ship to lie down. He fell fast asleep. 6The captain of the ship came and said, "Why are you sleeping? Get up! Pray to your god! Maybe your god will pay attention to us. Maybe he will save us!"

7Then the men said to each other, "Let's throw lots to see who caused these troubles to happen to us."

So the men threw lots. The lot showed that the trouble had happened because of Jonah.

¹²Jonah said to them, "Pick me up, and throw me into the sea. Then it will calm down. I know it is my fault that this great storm has come on you."

¹⁴So the men cried to the Lord, "Lord, please don't let us die because of taking this man's life. Please don't think we are guilty of killing an innocent man. Lord, you have caused all this to happen. You wanted it this way." ¹⁵Then the men picked up Jonah and threw him into the sea. So the sea became calm. ¹⁶Then they began to fear the Lord very much. They offered a sacrifice to the Lord. They also made promises to him.

¹⁷And the Lord caused a very big fish to swallow Jonah. Jonah was in the stomach of the fish three days and three nights.

[2:1] While Jonah was in the stomach of the fish, he prayed to the Lord his God. Jonah said,

2"I was in danger.

So I called to the Lord,

and he answered me.

I was about to die.

So I cried to you,

and you heard my voice.

3You threw me into the sea.

I went down, down into the deep sea.

The water was all around me.

Your powerful waves flowed over me.

6bBut you saved me from death,

Lord my God.

9"Lord, I will praise and thank you

while I give sacrifices to you.

I will make promises to you.

And I will do what I promise.

Salvation comes from the Lord!"

10Then the Lord spoke to the fish. And the fish spit Jonah out of its

stomach onto the dry land.

Wise Men from the East

(From Matthew 1 and 2)

[1:18] The mother of Jesus Christ was Mary. And this is how the birth of Jesus came about. Mary was engaged to marry Joseph. But before they married, she learned that she was going to have a baby. She was pregnant by the power of the Holy Spirit.

20b An angel of the Lord came to [Joseph] in a dream. The angel said, "Joseph, descendant of David, don't be afraid to take Mary as your wife. The baby in her is from the Holy Spirit. 21She will give

birth to a son. You will name the son Jesus. Give him that name because he will save his people from their sins."

²⁴When Joseph woke up, he did what the Lord's angel had told him to do. Joseph married Mary.

[2:1] Jesus was born in the town of Bethlehem in Judea during the time when Herod was king. After Jesus was born, some wise men from the east came to Jerusalem. ²They asked, "Where is the baby who was born to be the king of the Jews? We saw his star in the east. We came to worship him."

³When King Herod heard about this new king of the Jews, he was troubled. And all the people in Jerusalem were worried too. ⁴Herod called a meeting of all the leading priests and teachers of the law. He asked them where the Christ would be born. ⁵They

answered, "In the town of Bethlehem in Judea. The prophet wrote about this in the Scriptures:

6'But you, Bethlehem, in the land of Judah,
you are important among the rulers of Judah.
A ruler will come from you.
He will be like a shepherd for my people, the
Israelites.'"

7Then Herod had a secret meeting with the wise men from the east. He learned from them the exact time they first saw the star. 8Then Herod sent the wise men to Bethlehem. He said to them, "Go and look carefully to find the child. When you find him, come tell me. Then I can go worship him too."

[9]The wise men heard the king and then left. They saw the same star they had seen in the east. It went before them until it stopped above the place where the child was. [10]When the wise men saw the star, they were filled with joy. [11]They went to the house where the child was and saw him with his mother, Mary. They bowed down and worshiped the child. They opened the gifts they brought for him. They gave him treasures of gold, frankincense, and myrrh. [12]But God warned the wise men in a dream not to go back to Herod. So they went home to their own country by a different way.

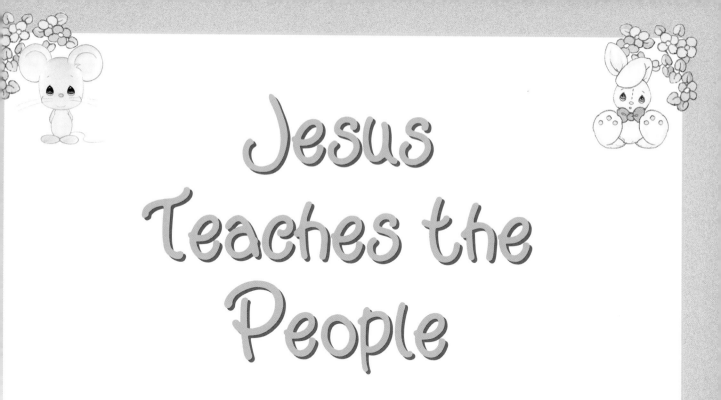

Jesus Teaches the People

(From Matthew 6 and 7)

[6:7] "And when you pray, don't be like those people who don't know God. They continue saying things that mean nothing. They think that God will hear them because of the many things they say. 8Don't be like them. Your Father knows the things you need before you ask him. 9So when you pray, you should pray like this:

'Our Father in heaven,

we pray that your name will always be kept holy.

¹⁰We pray that your kingdom will come.

We pray that what you want will be done,

here on earth as it is in heaven.

¹¹Give us the food we need for each day.

¹²Forgive the sins we have done,

just as we have forgiven those who did wrong to us.

¹³Do not cause us to be tested;

but save us from the Evil One.'

¹⁴Yes, if you forgive others for the things they do wrong, then your Father in heaven will also forgive you for the things you do wrong.

¹⁹"Don't store treasures for yourselves here on earth. Moths and rust will destroy treasures here on earth. And thieves can break

into your house and steal the things you have. [20]So store your treasure in heaven. The treasures in heaven cannot be destroyed by moths or rust. And thieves cannot break in and steal that treasure. [21]Your heart will be where your treasure is.

[25]"So I tell you, don't worry about the food you need to live. And don't worry about the clothes you need for your body.

[33]"The thing you should want most is God's kingdom and doing what God wants. Then all these other things you need will be given to you.

[7:12] "Do for other people the same things you want them to do for you. This is the meaning of the law of Moses and the teaching of the prophets."

Jesus Tells Stories

(From Matthew 13)

[13:3b] [Jesus] said: "A farmer went out to plant his seed. ⁴While he was planting, some seed fell by the road. The birds came and ate all that seed. ⁵Some seed fell on rocky ground, where there wasn't enough dirt. That seed grew very fast, because the ground was not deep. ⁶But when the sun rose, the plants dried up because they did not have deep roots. ⁷Some other seed fell among thorny weeds. The weeds grew and choked the good plants. ⁸ᵃSome other seed fell on good ground where it grew and became grain.

¹⁹"What is the seed that fell by the road? That seed is like the person who hears the teaching about the kingdom but does not understand it. The Evil One comes and takes away the things that were planted in that person's heart. ²⁰And what is the seed that fell on rocky ground? That seed is like the person who hears the teaching and quickly accepts it with joy. ²¹But he does not let the teaching go deep into his life. . . . When trouble or persecution comes because of the teaching he accepted, then he quickly gives up. ²²ᵃAnd what is the seed that fell among the thorny weeds? That seed is like the person who hears the teaching but lets worries about this life and love of money stop that teaching from growing. ²³ᵃBut what is the seed that fell on the good ground? That seed is like the person who hears the teaching and understands it. That person grows and produces fruit."

²⁴Then Jesus told them another story. He said, "The kingdom of heaven is like a man who planted good seed in his field. ²⁵That night, when everyone was asleep, his enemy came and planted weeds among the wheat. Then the enemy went away. ²⁶Later, the wheat grew and heads of grain grew on the wheat plants. But at the same time the weeds also grew. ^{28b}The servants asked, 'Do you want us to pull up the weeds?' ²⁹The man answered, 'No, because when you pull up the weeds, you might also pull up the wheat. ³⁰Let the weeds and the wheat grow together until the harvest time. At harvest time . . . gather the weeds and tie them together to be burned. Then gather the wheat and bring it to my barn.'"

³⁷Jesus [said to his disciples], "The man who planted the good seed in the field is the Son of Man. ³⁸The field is the world. And the good seed are all of God's children. . . . The weeds are those people

177

who belong to the Evil One. [39]And the enemy who planted the bad seed is the devil. The harvest time is the end of the world. And the workers who gather are God's angels.

[40b]"It will be this way at the end of the world. [41]The Son of Man will send out his angels. They will gather out of his kingdom all who cause sin and all who do evil. [43]Then the good people will shine like the sun in the kingdom of their Father. You people who hear me, listen!"

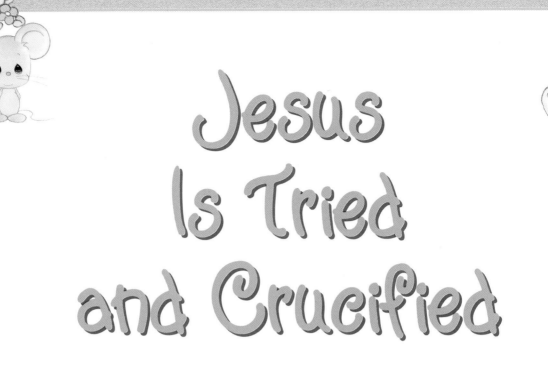

Jesus Is Tried and Crucified

(From Matthew 27)

[27:1] Early the next morning, all the leading priests and older leaders of the people decided to kill Jesus. ²They tied him, led him away, and turned him over to Pilate, the governor.

¹¹Jesus stood before Pilate. . . . Pilate asked him, "Are you the King of the Jews?"

Jesus answered, "Yes, I am."

¹²When the leading priests and the older leaders accused Jesus, he said nothing.

¹³So Pilate said to Jesus, "Don't you hear these people accusing you of all these things?"

¹⁴But Jesus said nothing in answer to Pilate. Pilate was very surprised at this.

¹⁵Every year at the time of Passover the governor would free one person from prison. This was always a person the people wanted to be set free. ¹⁶At that time there was a man in prison who was known to be very bad. His name was Barabbas. ¹⁷ᵇPilate said, "Which man do you want me to free: Barabbas, or Jesus who is called the Christ?"

²⁰But the leading priests and older leaders told the crowd to ask for Barabbas to be freed and for Jesus to be killed.

²¹Pilate said, "I have Barabbas and Jesus. Which do you want me to set free for you?"

The people answered, "Barabbas!"

²²Pilate asked, "What should I do with Jesus, the one called the Christ?"

They all answered, "Kill him on a cross!"

²⁴Pilate saw that he could do nothing about this, and a riot was starting. So he took some water and washed his hands in front of the crowd. Then he said, "I am not guilty of this man's death. You are the ones who are causing it!"

²⁶Then Pilate freed Barabbas. Pilate told some of the soldiers to beat Jesus with whips. Then he gave Jesus to the soldiers to be killed on a cross.

³²The soldiers were going out of the city with Jesus. They forced another man to carry the cross to be used for Jesus. This man was Simon, from Cyrene. ³³They all came to the place called Golgotha. (Golgotha means the Place of the Skull.) ³⁵The soldiers nailed Jesus to a cross. They threw lots to decide who would get his clothes. ³⁶The soldiers sat there and continued watching him. ³⁷They put a sign above Jesus' head with the charge against him written on it. The sign read: "THIS IS JESUS, THE KING OF THE JEWS."

⁴⁵At noon the whole country became dark. This darkness lasted for three hours. ⁴⁶About three o'clock Jesus cried out in a loud voice, " . . . My God, my God, why have you left me alone?"

⁵⁰Again Jesus cried out in a loud voice. Then he died.

⁵¹Then the curtain in the Temple split into two pieces. . . . Also, the earth shook and rocks broke apart.

⁵⁴The army officer and the soldiers guarding Jesus saw this earthquake and everything else that happened. They were very frightened and said, "He really was the Son of God!"

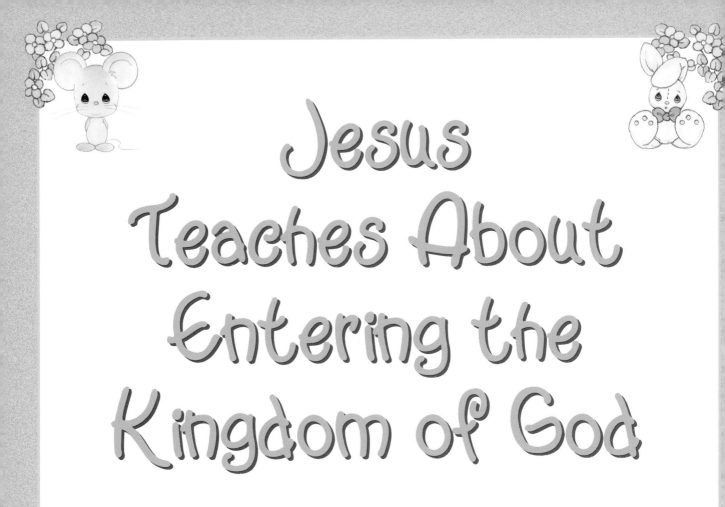

Jesus Teaches About Entering the Kingdom of God

(From Mark 10)

[10:13] Some people brought their small children to Jesus so he could touch them. But his followers told the people to stop bringing their children to him. 14When Jesus saw this, he was displeased. He said to them, "Let the little children come to me. Don't

stop them. The kingdom of God belongs to people who are like these little children. ¹⁵I tell you the truth. You must accept the kingdom of God as a little child accepts things, or you will never enter it." ¹⁶Then Jesus took the children in his arms. He put his hands on them and blessed them.

¹⁷Jesus started to leave, but a man ran to him and fell on his knees before Jesus. The man asked, "Good teacher, what must I do to get the life that never ends?"

¹⁸Jesus answered, "Why do you call me good? No one is good except God alone. ¹⁹You know the commands: 'You must not murder anyone. You must not be guilty of adultery. You must not steal. You must not tell lies about your neighbor in court. You must not cheat. Honor your father and mother.'"

²⁰The man said, "Teacher, I have obeyed all these commands since I was a boy."

²¹Jesus looked straight at the man and loved him. Jesus said, "There is still one more thing you need to do. Go and sell everything you have, and give the money to the poor. You will have a reward in heaven. Then come and follow me."

²²He was very sad to hear Jesus say this, and he left. The man was sad because he was very rich.

²³Then Jesus looked at his followers and said, "How hard it will be for those who are rich to enter the kingdom of God!"

²⁴The followers were amazed at what Jesus said. But he said again, "My children, it is very hard to enter the kingdom of God! ²⁵And it

will be very hard for a rich person to enter the kingdom of God. It would be easier for a camel to go through the eye of a needle!"

26The followers were even more amazed and said to each other, "Then who can be saved?"

27Jesus looked straight at them and said, "This is something that men cannot do. But God can do it. God can do all things."

Jesus Heals on the Sabbath and Teaches with Stories

(From Luke 13—15)

[13:10] Jesus was teaching in one of the synagogues on the Sabbath day. ¹¹In the synagogue there was a woman who had an evil spirit in her. This spirit had made the woman a cripple for 18 years. Her back was always bent; she could not stand up straight. ¹²When

Jesus saw her, he called her over and said, "Woman, your sickness has left you!" ¹³Jesus put his hands on her. Immediately she was able to stand up straight and began praising God.

¹⁴The synagogue leader was angry because Jesus healed on the Sabbath day. He said to the people, "There are six days for work. So come to be healed on one of those days. . . . ."

¹⁵The Lord answered, "You people are hypocrites! All of you untie your work animals and lead them to drink water every day—even on the Sabbath day! ¹⁶This woman that I healed is our Jewish sister. . . . Surely it is not wrong for her to be freed from her sickness on a Sabbath day!" ¹⁷When Jesus said this, all the men who were criticizing him were ashamed. And all the people were happy for the wonderful things Jesus was doing.

[14:1] On a Sabbath day, Jesus went to the home of a leading Pharisee to eat with him. The people there were all watching Jesus very closely. ²A man with dropsy was brought before Jesus. ³Jesus said to the Pharisees and teachers of the law, "Is it right or wrong to heal on the Sabbath day?" ⁴But they would not answer his question. So Jesus took the man, healed him, and sent him away.

[15:1] Many tax collectors and "sinners" came to listen to Jesus. ²The Pharisees and the teachers of the law began to complain: "Look! This man welcomes sinners and even eats with them!"

³Then Jesus told them this story: ⁴"Suppose one of you has 100 sheep, but he loses 1 of them. Then he will leave the other 99 sheep alone and go out and look for the lost sheep. The man will keep on searching for the lost sheep until he finds it. ⁵And when he finds it, the man is very happy. He puts it on his shoulders ⁶and goes

home. He calls to his friends and neighbors and says, 'Be happy with me because I found my lost sheep!' [7]In the same way, I tell you there is much joy in heaven when 1 sinner changes his heart. There is more joy for that 1 sinner than there is for 99 good people who don't need to change.

[8]"Suppose a woman has ten silver coins, but she loses one of them. She will light a lamp and clean the house. She will look carefully for the coin until she finds it. [9]And when she finds it, she will call her friends and neighbors and say, 'Be happy with me because I have found the coin that I lost!' [10]In the same way, there is joy before the angels of God when 1 sinner changes his heart."

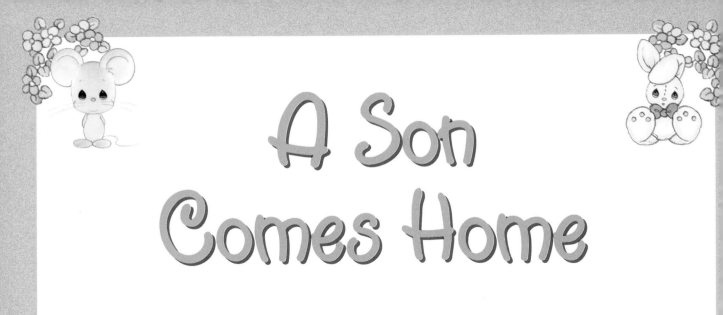

A Son Comes Home

(From Luke 15)

[15:11] Then Jesus said, "A man had two sons. ¹²The younger son said to his father, 'Give me my share of the property.' So the father divided the property between his two sons. ¹³Then the younger son gathered up all that was his and left. He traveled far away to another country. There he wasted his money in foolish living. ¹⁴ᵇSoon after that, the land became very dry, and there was no rain. There was not enough food to eat anywhere in the country. The son was hungry and needed money. ¹⁵So he got a job . . . feed[ing] pigs. ¹⁶The son was so hungry that he was willing to eat the food

the pigs were eating. But no one gave him anything. [17]The son realized that he had been very foolish. He thought, 'All of my father's servants have plenty of food. But I am here, almost dying with hunger. [18]I will leave and return to my father. I'll say to him: Father, I have sinned against God and have done wrong to you. [19]I am not good enough to be called your son. But let me be like one of your servants.' [20]So the son left and went to his father.

"While the son was still a long way off, his father saw him coming. He felt sorry for his son. So the father ran to him, and hugged and kissed him. [21]The son said, 'Father, I have sinned against God and have done wrong to you. I am not good enough to be called your son.' [22]But the father said to his servants, 'Hurry! Bring the best clothes and put them on him. Also, put a ring on his finger and sandals on his feet. [23]And get our fat calf and kill it. Then we can

have a feast and celebrate! ²⁴My son was dead, but now he is alive again! He was lost, but now he is found!' So they began to celebrate.

²⁵"The older son was in the field. As he came closer to the house, he heard the sound of music and dancing. ²⁶So he called to one of the servants and asked, 'What does all this mean?' ²⁷The servant said, 'Your brother has come back. Your father killed the fat calf to eat because your brother came home safely!' ²⁸The older son was angry and would not go in to the feast. So his father went out and begged him to come in. ²⁹The son said to his father, 'I have served you like a slave for many years! I have always obeyed your commands. But you never even killed a young goat for me to have a feast with my friends. ³⁰But your other son has wasted all your money. . . . Then he comes home, and you kill the fat calf for

him!' ³¹The father said to him, 'Son, you are always with me. All that I have is yours. ³²We had to celebrate and be happy because your brother was dead, but now he is alive. He was lost, but now he is found.'"

The Greatest Gift

(From John 3)

[3:16] "For God loved the world so much that he gave his only Son. God gave his Son so that whoever believes in him may not be lost, but have eternal life. [17]God did not send his Son into the world to judge the world guilty, but to save the world through him. [18]He who believes in God's Son is not judged guilty. He who does not believe has already been judged guilty, because he has not believed in God's only Son. [19]People are judged by this fact: I am the Light from God that has come into the world. But men did not want light. They wanted darkness because they were doing

evil things. [20]Everyone who does evil hates the light. He will not come to the light because it will show all the evil things he has done. [21]But he who follows the true way comes to the light. Then the light will show that the things he has done were done through God."

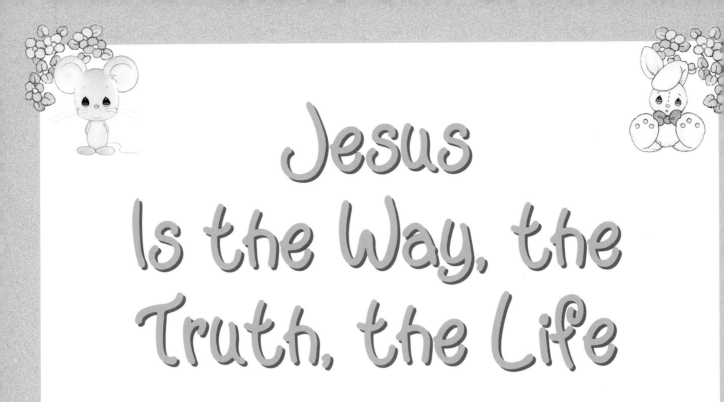

Jesus Is the Way, the Truth, the Life

(From John 14)

[14:1] Jesus said, "Don't let your hearts be troubled. Trust in God. And trust in me. ²There are many rooms in my Father's house. I would not tell you this if it were not true. I am going there to prepare a place for you. ³After I go and prepare a place for you, I will come back. Then I will take you to be with me so that you may be where I am. ⁴You know the way to the place where I am going."

[5]Thomas said to Jesus, "Lord, we don't know where you are going. So how can we know the way?"

[6]Jesus answered, "I am the way. And I am the truth and the life. The only way to the Father is through me."

Love Each Other

(From John 15)

[15:9] "I loved you as the Father loved me. Now remain in my love. ¹⁰I have obeyed my Father's commands, and I remain in his love. In the same way, if you obey my commands, you will remain in my love. ¹¹I have told you these things so that you can have the same joy I have. I want your joy to be the fullest joy.

¹²"This is my command: Love each other as I have loved you. ¹³The greatest love a person can show is to die for his friends. ¹⁴You are my friends if you do what I command you. ¹⁵I don't call you

servants now. A servant does not know what his master is doing. But now I call you friends because I have made known to you everything I heard from my Father. ¹⁶You did not choose me; I chose you. And I gave you this work, to go and produce fruit. I want you to produce fruit that will last. Then the Father will give you anything you ask for in my name. ¹⁷This is my command: Love each other."

Love Is Patient

(From 1 Corinthians 13)

[13:1] I may speak in different languages of men or even angels. But if I do not have love, then I am only a noisy bell or a ringing cymbal. ²I may have the gift of prophecy; I may understand all the secret things of God and all knowledge; and I may have faith so great that I can move mountains. But even with all these things, if I do not have love, then I am nothing. ³I may give everything I have to feed the poor. And I may even give my body as an offering to be burned. But I gain nothing by doing these things if I do not have love.

⁴Love is patient and kind. Love is not jealous, it does not brag, and it is not proud. ⁵Love is not rude, is not selfish, and does not become angry easily. Love does not remember wrongs done against it. ⁶Love is not happy with evil, but is happy with the truth. ⁷Love patiently accepts all things. It always trusts, always hopes, and always continues strong.

⁸Love never ends. There are gifts of prophecy, but they will be ended. There are gifts of speaking in different languages, but those gifts will end. There is the gift of knowledge, but it will be ended. ⁹These things will end, because this knowledge and those prophecies we have are not complete. ¹⁰But when perfection comes, the things that are not complete will end. ¹¹When I was a child, I talked like a child; I thought like a child; I made plans like a child. When I became a man, I stopped those childish ways. ¹²It is the

same with us. Now we see as if we are looking into a dark mirror. But at that time, in the future, we shall see clearly. Now I know only a part. But at that time I will know fully, as God has known me. [13]So these three things continue forever: faith, hope and love. And the greatest of these is love.

The Full Armor of God

(From Ephesians 6)

[6:10] Finally, be strong in the Lord and in his great power. [11]Wear the full armor of God. Wear God's armor so that you can fight against the devil's evil tricks. [12]Our fight is not against people on earth. We are fighting against the rulers and authorities and the powers of this world's darkness. We are fighting against the spiritual powers of evil in the heavenly world. [13]That is why you need to get God's full armor. Then on the day of evil you will be able to stand strong. And when you have finished the whole fight, you will

still be standing. ¹⁴So stand strong, with the belt of truth tied around your waist. And on your chest wear the protection of right living. ¹⁵And on your feet wear the Good News of peace to help you stand strong. ¹⁶And also use the shield of faith. With that you can stop all the burning arrows of the Evil One. ¹⁷Accept God's salvation to be your helmet. And take the sword of the Spirit—that sword is the teaching of God. ¹⁸Pray in the Spirit at all times. Pray with all kinds of prayers, and ask for everything you need. To do this you must always be ready. Never give up. Always pray for all God's people.

¹⁹Also pray for me. Pray that when I speak, God will give me words so that I can tell the secret truth of the Good News without fear. ²⁰I have the work of speaking that Good News. I am doing that now, here in prison. Pray that when I preach the Good News I will speak without fear, as I should.

faith in Jesus

(From 1 Peter 1)

[1:3] Praise be to the God and Father of our Lord Jesus Christ. God has great mercy, and because of his mercy he gave us a new life. He gave us a living hope because Jesus Christ rose from death. ⁴Now we hope for the blessings God has for his children. These blessings are kept for you in heaven. They cannot be destroyed or be spoiled or lose their beauty. ⁵God's power protects you through your faith, and it keeps you safe until your salvation comes. That salvation is ready to be given to you at the end of time. ⁶This

makes you very happy. But now for a short time different kinds of troubles may make you sad. ⁷These troubles come to prove that your faith is pure. This purity of faith is worth more than gold. Gold can be proved to be pure by fire, but gold will ruin. But the purity of your faith will bring you praise and glory and honor when Jesus Christ comes again. ⁸You have not seen Christ, but still you love him. You cannot see him now, but you believe in him. You are filled with a joy that cannot be explained. And that joy is full of glory. ⁹Your faith has a goal, to save your souls. And you are receiving that goal—your salvation.

¹⁰The prophets searched carefully and tried to learn about this salvation. They spoke about the grace that was coming to you. ¹¹The Spirit of Christ was in the prophets. And the Spirit was telling about the sufferings that would happen to Christ and about the

glory that would come after those sufferings. The prophets tried to learn about what the Spirit was showing them. They tried to learn when those things would happen and what the world would be like at that time. [12]It was shown to them that their service was not for themselves. It was for you. They were serving you when they told about the truths you have now heard. The men who preached the Good News to you told you those things. They did it with the help of the Holy Spirit that was sent from heaven. These are truths that even the angels want very much to know about.

The King of Kings

(From Revelation 21 and 22)

[21:1] Then I saw a new heaven and a new earth. The first heaven and the first earth had disappeared. Now there was no sea. ²And I saw the holy city coming down out of heaven from God. This holy city is the new Jerusalem. It was prepared like a bride dressed for her husband. ³I heard a loud voice from the throne. The voice said, "Now God's home is with men. He will live with them, and they will be his people. God himself will be with them and will be their God. ⁴He will wipe away every tear from their eyes. There will be

no more death, sadness, crying, or pain. All the old ways are gone."

¹⁰The angel carried me away by the Spirit to a very large and high mountain. He showed me the holy city, Jerusalem. It was coming down out of heaven from God. ¹¹It was shining with the glory of

God. It was shining bright like a very expensive jewel, like a jasper. It was clear as crystal.

[22:12] "Listen! I am coming soon! I will bring rewards with me. I will repay each one for what he has done. [13]I am the Alpha and the Omega, the First and the Last, the Beginning and the End.

16"I, Jesus, have sent my angel to tell you these things for the churches. I am the descendant from the family of David. I am the bright morning star."

17The Spirit and the bride say, "Come!" Everyone who hears this should also say, "Come!" If anyone is thirsty, let him come; whoever wishes it may have the water of life as a free gift.

20Jesus is the One who says that these things are true. Now he says, "Yes, I am coming soon."

Amen. Come, Lord Jesus!

21The grace of the Lord Jesus be with all. Amen.

Songs
and
Prayers

The B-I-B-L-E

The B-I-B-L-E!

Yes, that's the Book for me.

I stand alone on the Word of God,

The B-I-B-L-E!

Jesus Loves the Little Children

Jesus loves the little children,

All the children of the world.

Red and yellow, black, and white,

They are precious in His sight.

Jesus loves the little children of the world.

Jesus Loves Me

Jesus loves me, this I know,

For the Bible tells me so;

Little ones to Him belong,

They are weak, but He is strong.

Yes, Jesus loves me!

Yes, Jesus loves me!

Yes, Jesus loves me!

The Bible tells me so.

—Anna B. Warner

Amazing Grace

Amazing grace, how sweet the sound,

That saved a wretch like me!

I once was lost, but now am found,

Was blind but now I see.

—*John Newton*

Prayers

May the love of God our Father

Be in all our homes today;

May the love of the Lord Jesus

Keep our hearts and minds always;

May his loving Holy Spirit

Guide and bless the ones I love,

Father, mother, brothers, sisters,

Keep them safely in His love.

—*Unknown*

Thank You, Lord, for giving me

A happy, caring family.

Thank You for the friends I meet,

And for the neighbors down the street;

But most of all, dear Lord above,

I thank You for Your precious love.

—Unknown

Lord, make me an instrument of your peace.

Where there is hatred, let me sow love,

Where there is injury, pardon,

Where there is despair, hope,

Where there is darkness, light,

Where there is sadness, joy.

—St. Francis of Assisi

God is great, and God is good.

Let us thank Him for our food.

By His hand we all are fed;

Thank You, Lord, for our daily bread.

Now I lay me down to sleep.

I pray You, Lord, my soul to keep.

Your love be with me through the night

And wake me with the morning light.

—Traditional

A Prayer from Someone Who Loves Me . . .

_____

_____

_____

_____

_____

_____

My Own Bedtime Prayer . . .

_____

_____

_____

_____

_____

_____